What are...?

GEYSERS

Claire Llewellyn

Heinemann

For more information about Heinemann Library books, or to order, please telephone +44 (0)1865 888066, or send a fax to +44 (0)1865 314091. You can visit our web site at www.heinemann.co.uk

First published in Great Britain by Heinemann Library,
Halley Court, Jordan Hill, Oxford OX2 8EJ
a division of Reed Educational and Professional Publishing Ltd.
Heinemann is a registered trademark of Reed Educational & Professional Publishing Ltd.

OXFORD MELBOURNE AUCKLAND
JOHANNESBURG BLANTYRE GABORONE
IBADAN PORTSMOUTH (NH) USA CHICAGO

Designed by David Oakley
Illustrations by Hardlines (p.8) and Jo Brooker
Printed by South China Printing Co.(1988) Ltd, Hong Kong / China

05 04 03 02 01
10 9 8 7 6 5 4 3 2 1

ISBN 0 431 02386 7

British Library Cataloguing in Publication Data
This book is also available in a hardback library edition (ISBN 0 431 02380 8)

Llewellyn, Claire
  What are geysers?
  1. Geysers – Juvenile literature
  1. Title II. Geysers
  551.2'3

Acknowledgements
The Publishers would like to thank the following for permission to reproduce photographs:
Bruce Coleman: Gunter Ziesler p.18; FLPA: David Hosking p.7, p.10, p.11, Winifried Wisniewski p.12, NASA: Johnson Space Centre p.22, p.24; Oxford Scientific Films: Stan Osolonski p.4, James Robinson p.5, T Middleton p.6, Richard Packwood p.9, Norbert Rosing p.28; Peter Arnold Inc: Jim Wark p.26; Still Pictures: Hjalte Tin p.13, p.16, Jim Wark p.14, B&C Alexander p.15, Yves Thonnerieux p.17, Steve Kaufman p.19, Massimo Lupioi p.20, Andre Maslennieov p.21; Telegraph Colour Library: V.C.L p.29.

Cover photograph reproduced with permission of Robert Harding Picture Library.

Every effort has been made to contact copyright holders of any material reproduced in this book. Any omissions will be rectified in subsequent printings if notice is given to the Publisher.

Contents

Some words are shown in bold, **like this**.
You can find out what they mean by looking
in the Glossary.

What is a geyser?

A geyser is a **jet** of boiling water and steam that **erupts** out of the ground. It can shoot high up into the air.

This geyser shoots boiling water about 30 metres above the ground.

A geyser sinks back down into a hole in the ground.

Most geysers last for a few minutes and then sink back down to the ground. Some geysers erupt again a few minutes or hours later. Others may erupt after several weeks.

Geysers and volcanoes

Geysers are found in the same parts of the world as **active volcanoes**. Most geysers are found in New Zealand, Iceland and the USA.

Geysers are found where volcanoes heat up the ground

'Old Faithful' erupts once an hour.

'Old Faithful' is a geyser in Yellowstone
National Park in the USA. Many people
go there to watch it erupt.

How are geysers made?

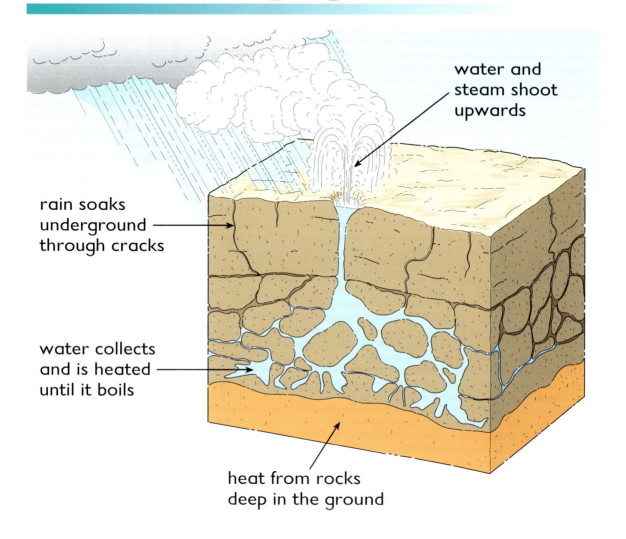

water and steam shoot upwards

rain soaks underground through cracks

water collects and is heated until it boils

heat from rocks deep in the ground

The water in a geyser starts as rain. The rain runs down through cracks in the ground and collects in spaces between the rocks.

Bubbling, boiling water shoots up out of the ground.

Near **volcanoes**, the rocks are very hot. Underground, the water begins to boil. It bubbles up through cracks in the rock and **erupts** as a geyser.

From water to stone

Underground, the hot water **dissolves** the rock around it. Because of this, geyser water contains many tiny pieces of rock called **minerals**.

These steps were made from minerals in the geyser water.

Minerals pile up in many different shapes.

Above the ground, the geyser water cools, and the minerals pile up on the ground. This is rather like the white powder that builds up in kettles and saucepans.

Geysers in Iceland

There are many geysers in Iceland. Iceland is a very cold country, and parts of it are covered with ice.

Hot geysers can keep the ground around them clear of ice.

Sometimes geysers can erupt onto ice. Then the hot water melts the ice. Streams of water pour downhill, and can cause floods.

This water may start a flood when it reaches flat land.

Hot springs

In some places the hot water under the ground does not boil and shoot out as a geyser. It flows out more gently as a **hot spring**. They are sometimes very bright colours because they are full of **minerals**.

Hot springs run into this pool in Yellowstone **National Park**.

People like to sit in these hot springs in Iceland.

Some people believe that the minerals in the hot springs are good for their bones and they like to soak in the water.

Steam and mud

Hot steam comes out of the ground near **volcanoes**.

In some places near hot springs and geysers, small clouds of steam hiss out of the ground.

In other places, steam and hot water bubble up through a layer of clay. The water and clay mix together to make a hot mud-pool.

This bubbling, hot mud-pool is in Iceland.

Winter warmth

Geysers shoot out hot water all year round. This stops nearby rivers and pools freezing over in cold weather. Birds can feed in them all winter long.

Canada geese feed on plants and animals in this pool.

These Japanese monkeys spend a lot of time sitting in **hot springs**.

In the mountains of Japan, the winters are very cold. Monkeys keep themselves warm by bathing in the hot springs.

Using geysers

Geysers give us energy that we can use.
The hot water can be piped to swimming pools
and homes. It can be used to heat greenhouses.

These bananas are growing
in a greenhouse in Iceland.

The **jet** of steam helps to drive the machines.

A geyser's hot jet of steam can be used to make electricity. It is a clean and cheap way to make it. This power station in Iceland makes electricity from nearby geysers.

Geyser map 1

This photo shows part of the Yellowstone **National Park** in the USA. It was taken from a satellite. You can see Yellowstone Lake in the middle. There are high mountains around the lake. They are covered with snow.

Key

▨ lake		low land	
〜 mountains		snow	

Maps are pictures of the land. This map shows us the same place as the photo. The brown colour shows the land. The wiggly lines show the mountains.

Geyser map 2

This photo shows a smaller area of the park. You can see Yellowstone Lake in the middle. You can also see a river flowing into the the lake at the bottom right of the picture.

Key

	lake		mountains		low land	
	rivers		geyser area			

The key on the map tells us what the colours mean. The river is easy to see on the map. It is a thin green line. The purple blob shows where all the geysers and **hot springs** are.

Geyser map 3

This photo shows the geyser area of Yellowstone **National Park**. It was taken from an aeroplane. You can see the bright colours of the **hot springs**. They are in the area where the geysers **erupt**.

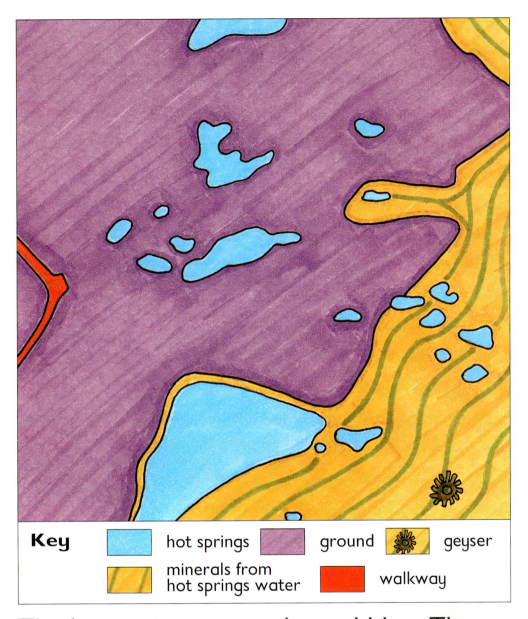

Key		hot springs		ground		geyser
		minerals from hot springs water				walkway

The hot springs are coloured blue. The **minerals** which have come out of the hot springs are coloured stripey orange. On the left of the map you can see a walkway where people can watch the geysers.

Amazing geyser facts

'Old Faithful' shoots out 55,000 litres (12,000 gallons) of water each time it **erupts**. That's enough to fill a small swimming pool!

This is Mount Tarawera now.

The highest-ever geyser was near Mount Tarawera in New Zealand. It once shot up 460 metres — that's higher than the Eiffel Tower (320 metres)!

Glossary

active a volcano that is able to erupt

dissolve to disappear in hot water, like sugar in tea

erupt to suddenly shoot out hot water and steam

jet a very strong stream or gush of water

hot spring warm water that bubbles gently up out of the ground

mineral the hard, tiny grains from which rocks are made

National Park a piece of land that is protected by law to keep it safe

satellite a special machine that goes around the Earth in space. It can take photographs of the Earth

volcano a mountain that is still being made. It sometimes erupts, shooting out hot rock and ash from inside the Earth.

More books to read

Daniel Rogers. *Geography Starts Here! Volcano.*
Wayland, 1998

Claire Llewellyn.
Why do we have ...Rocks and Mountains?
Heinemann, 1997

Index